C000053402

IMAGES
*of England*

# EASTON AND EASTVILLE

The originator of the Easton publications – the author's uncle, Lionel Ellery, holds aloft the St Mark's book which started it all.

IMAGES
*of England*

# EASTON AND EASTVILLE

*Compiled by*
Veronica Smith

TEMPUS

First published 2001
Copyright © Veronica Smith, 2001

Tempus Publishing Limited
The Mill, Brimscombe Port,
Stroud, Gloucestershire, GL5 2QG

ISBN 0 7524 2237 5

Typesetting and origination by
Tempus Publishing Limited
Printed in Great Britain by
Midway Colour Print, Wiltshire

*I should like to dedicate this book to the memory of my very dear friend Iris Warn and to Steven Jenkins the son of another very dear friend: constantly remembered at unexpected moments.*

An early snap of the author with her grandmother in the garden. Perkins building can be seen behind the wall; as can most of the garden which was given over to poultry keeping.

# Contents

The wedding of Susan Hopton to George Ford 1962. Her sisters Margaret and Christine were bridesmaids, as was the author. Two years later the couple emigrated to America. George died in 1990.

# Introduction

Some folk seem amazed I can find anything new to say about East Bristol but information and photographs come constantly into my possession revealing facts of which I was unaware and some I once knew but had forgotten. To me there is a fascination in peeling away the layers of time to reveal details of people who, in days long past, trod the same streets, experienced joy and sadness or sometimes just plain old boredom. They may have led very different lives from today's residents but their feelings and reactions must have been just the same.

Changes in life styles and even our surroundings are so gradual as to be imperceptible. Walking down Warwick Road recently I suddenly noticed the cluster of chimneys on one of the Georgian houses in Stapleton Road and thought what a rarity it was to see a chimney these days. It was the same with the demolition of so many streets – it didn't happen overnight – terraces just began to dwindle. I noticed yesterday that the last little derelict shops in Lower Ashley Road have wire fencing round them so clearly their cards have been marked.

My preoccupation with the past has long been apparent. As a child I ceaselessly questioned my mother about pre-war days which, fortunately, she enjoyed describing. I was like a blotter, absorbing all the information she could provide. I yearned so much to go back in time and see it all for myself, that writing about it has been some kind of outlet for this consuming desire for knowledge. I spend hours pouring over old directories and actually pacing the streets locating exact positions of shops and houses which is fine unless they happen to have been properties now buried under Easton Way – then it can be a bit hazardous!

This book has been arranged in parishes. I have to warn now that in some instances I have crossed the border into the next parish but boundaries are nebulous lines anyway, varying as to church or council. Try and think of my chapter divisions as circles which overlap in places.

I hope you enjoy the book and it brings back happy recollections to all of you. Thank you all for sharing my interest in days gone by.

Veronica Smith
June 2001

# Acknowledgements

My thanks to everyone who has shared their memories with me. Special appreciation is given to those who have loaned me precious photographs and taken the trouble to provide me with names, locations and all the interesting information which turns a collection of photographs into a social document. Gratitude therefore goes to: Sylvia Ballinger, Rosa Brewer, Bristol Co-operative Society Archives, *Bristol Evening Post*, David Caseley, Grace Cooper, Arthur Cotter, Doreen Cowley, Jean Cowley, Stella Davies, Colin Downs, Mervyn Ellery, Pamela Fursman, Richard Haines, Patsy Hammond, Margaret and Dave Harris, Brian Heyward, Abdul Ismail, Emma Knight, Ann Lawrence, Mollie Maby, Barbara Marsh, Sue Morton, Michael Mott, Leslie Norman, Charles Randall, Doreen Redmore, Ralph Robbins, Dennis Rugman, Margaret Smailes, Bob Stubbins, Doreen Taylor, Bill Thomas, Roger and Peter Tovey, Mike Tozer, David Tucker, Maureen Warner, Hilda Ward and Joan Ward, Terry Warren, Ivy Wilcox, Vi Wilcox.

# One
# St Simon's

*Anyone revisiting this area after an absence of forty years would find immense changes had taken place. Vast chunks of this district disappeared during the 1960s including the entire length of Pennywell Road. All the little shops, pubs and houses that lined the top part of Lower Ashley Road and Warwick Road were also swept away as well as all the streets which lay behind. There is a bleakness about the terrain now which never existed before with masses of properties all bunched together in a wonderful conglomerate of architectural styles. The whole character of this part of East Bristol has altered irrevocably.*

St Simon's church before it was bought by the Greek Orthodox clergy and prior to losing the top section of its spire, is seen here around 1899. The terrace of shops disappeared in the 1960s to make way for the Charlotte Keel Health Centre. At the time this picture was taken the traders were: No. 148 Orr and Pole, wholesale boot/shoe manufacturer; No. 146 William Clapp, pawnbroker; No. 144 premises shared by Robert Arnold, furniture broker and J.R. Jenkins, plumber; No. 142 James Stidstone, newsagents; No. 140 James Sullivan, removal business. The corner shop served as refreshment rooms whose proprietor was John Kinsman; the is the only shop which remains of this terrace and it is now an off licence run by Santosh Singh.

The interior of the church with its graceful arches and delicate rood screen *c.* 1920.

The Pound Day parade held at the church in the 1940s. Margaret Green is in the front wearing a pale hat and coat. It was a charitable event providing the needy with food parcels.

## Bristol Education Committee.

*Baptist Mills Inf.* **SCHOOL.**

**Presented to** *Ena Roberts*

Who was presented to H.M. INSPECTOR in Standard *IV*
on the *24th* day of *March* 190*4* , and
whose Conduct has been good and Attendance regular during the
preceding year.

School open *414* times. Attendance *412*

Signed *Geo. Bolam*

*Head Master*

An inscription from the flyleaf of a book presented to Ena Roberts of Baptist Mills School in 1904.

Mollie Fraser with classmates at
Baptist Mills school in the 1930s.

Mollie Fraser outside her uncle's pub, the Victoria which stood on the corner of Blenheim Street and Oxford Place. This photograph is from the 1940s, prior to the closing of the pub in the 1950s. All along this side of Blenheim Street was demolished to make way for Mill House sheltered accommodation.

Drinkers were spoiled for choice in this neighbourhood where pubs abounded. This was the Cornwallis on the Lower Ashley Road/Waverley Street corner. This land is now the playing fields of Millpond Primary School. The building on the right is the Warwick Arms. The railings of No. 187 can be seen on the left. These small enclosed paved areas were a popular feature at the time the houses were built. They were a great temptation to children who couldn't resist swinging on the corner post as they passed.

June 1953 and Mollie Ward and friends are taking part in a fancy dress parade at the Coronation party in Walpole Street. Clearance of these houses began in the mid-1960s but the street did not finally disappear until the early 1970s.

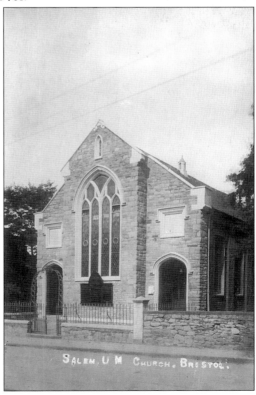

Salem United Methodist church which stood in Lower Ashley Road in the rank between Millpond Street and Waverley Road. Its grounds were quite extensive. It closed in the 1950s.

Many of the local girls worked at Brooks Dye Works and Laundry. These employees busily sorting piles of garments appear to have been photographed in the 1940s.

The White Lion was to be found at the junction of Millpond Street and Lower Ashley Road. It was demolished in the late 1960s and the Mill Community Centre built on the site.

On the corner of Lovell Street and Bean Street was the Bunch of Grapes off-licence. This was one of the first properties to be pulled down in the early 1960s at which time the licence was held by Mrs Kerchell. Easton Way now crosses this section of land.

The Beer Cask, No. 189 Pennywell Road. This was on the stretch of road between Bean Street and Green's Gully, where a tragic accident occured when a little boy ran headlong down the gully and died under the wheels of a passing vehicle. Mothers used this cautionary tale to warn their children of the dangers of not paying attention when playing near the roads.

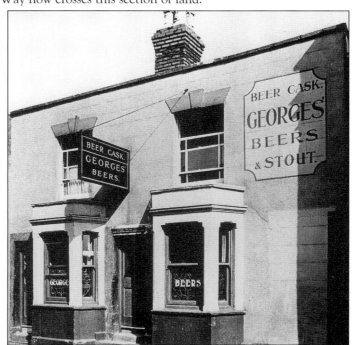

June 1964 and clearance is well under
way in Pennywell Road. These two
photographs show the front and rear of a
second hand shop trading to the bitter
end. This is the approximate site of the
present day Hathway Walk.

The living accommodation belonging to the shop on Pennywell Road as seen from Plumer Street in 1964.

James Preston, fellmongers, whose building was close to the Lower Ashley Road end of Pennywell Road, around 1964. They processed the skins collected from the nearby slaughterhouse. The busy M32 roundabout sweeps over this area today.

The Painters Arms, tucked away in Summers Road off Lower Ashley Road. This must have been taken not long before it was torn down in the 1960s. The name of the publican above the door is Elsie May Barefoot. Her late husband, Ernest, had run the pub since the 1920s. This sunlit scene seems to typify days from the past – tranquil times when a cat could lounge in peace on the pavement. You can almost smell the ale wafting from the bar. Nearby was another pub, appropriately called the Skinners Arms bearing in mind its proximity to the fellmongers.

Browning's cycle repair shop pictured in 1964 when it had already been standing empty for some years. Pennywell Road was an interesting mix of houses, industry and shops with a great variety of architectural styles, all of which could be studied at leisure from the windows of the single decker No. 139 bus.

Earlsmead Ale and Porter Stores stood at No. 144 Pennywell Road. It was pulled down, together with neighbouring properties, in the 1960s and industrial units were built on the site.

New maisonettes were already established in Pennywell Road (far left) around the late 1970s, while in the foreground is rubble from the demolished houses of Stapleton Road. This was the little terrace of shops which included Sid Purnell's original butcher's shop and a fabric store. In earlier days there had been a greengrocer's, a milliner's and J.H. Mills' grocery shop.

Bates Close has sprung up where King Street once stood. In June 1964 half the street had already been pulled down.

The rear of No. 11, empty and awaiting the demolition men in 1964.

Looking up King Street to Pennywell Road in the last months before all these buildings were swept away in 1964. Some interesting cars of the period are parked by the kerb.

Colston Place was situated between Nos 131 and 133 Pennywell Road. At the time of this photograph around 1919, on one corner was a grocery store run by William Thomas and, on the opposite corner, shown here, was an off-licence called The Fountain Head, also run by a William Thomas – they might perhaps have been father and son. It looks as if these residents from the early years of the twentieth century are preparing to depart for an outing.

Many years have passed and the off-licence has fallen into decay in this, the summer of 1964. The last owner, Mr Wilson, has received his compulsory purchase order and demolition is imminent.

September 1965 and the corner has been razed to the ground. The empty space is where Nos 103-131 once stood, and where Highett Drive and Barker Walk can now be found. Fiddes, the wholesale grocers, had traded here since the 1920s. They relocated to Easton Road onto the site now occupied by the Iceland Freezer centre.

The magnificent Beaumont Hotel which stood on the corner of Goodhind Street and Beaumont Terrace. In 1899 the landlord was Farnham Brimble, a suitable grandiose name for the licensee of a place of such architectural opulence. The houses seen in the background are those of Russell Street and behind the parked car is a small segment of Claremont Street.

Mr and Mrs Thomas, residents of Goodhind Street in the 1920s.

Mrs Thomas with her children, Ethel (Doreen) and Bill in the back garden of their house around the 1920s.

The Thomas children, again from the 1920s, pose patiently outside the front of their home but it is clear they are anxious to get on with their ball game.

# Two
# Trinity

*This is another area where colossal changes have taken place. There is an aridity about the area now with its soulless high rise flats, stark maisonettes and lack of shops in such contrast to the jumble of assorted buildings of days gone by. Perhaps the saddest aspect is the loss of so many manufacturing companies for local shopkeepers, who relied upon employees of these companies for much of their trade.*

MASSON SCOTT THRISSELL

The Masson Scott Thrissell plant seemed a permanent fixture amidst the disappearing streets around. The company had begun as Brecknell, Munro and Rogers Ltd, Brassfounders in the 1920s and by the mid-1930s had evolved into Thrissell Engineering, taking its name from the road where it was situated. This, in turn, was named after Thrissell House on Stapleton Road where Dr W.G. Grace had a surgery in the 1890s. Masson Scott Thrissell finally closed down in the late 1980s and an industrial park was built on the site.

Members of staff from when it was simply known as 'Thrissells'. This photograph is from the 1940s and seems to be a celebration of some sort.

Margaret Harris, Mrs Peggy Mayo and Janet Futcher around the 1960-1970s.

An office party, early 1960s. From left to right, back row: Mrs Peggy Mayo, Reg Ford, Les Haskins, -?-, Brenda Hodges, Albert Nurse, Diane Fry, Mr James. Front row: -?-, Rita Munro, Margaret Harris, Janet Futcher, Sue?

A pre-wedding do for Rita (seated) who was about to marry the footballer, Alex Munro, in the 1960s. From left to right, standing: Margaret Hoare, Janet Futcher, Brenda Hodges, Diane Fry.

Florence and Ellie Hiscocks outside their home in Zion Road in the 1920s. This little road led from Stapleton Road to Clarence Road. Little courts with names like Cottage Place and Norfolk Buildings led off this thoroughfare. The houses had all gone by the 1940s in favour of commercial properties. All that remains today is a pathway by the architectural salvage yard.

The Sceptre stood on the corner of Stapleton Road and Clifton Place around 1919. When this photograph was taken the landlord was Sam Bryant and members of his family can be seen in the second doorway. I remember sitting in Jones' restaurant on the opposite side of Stapleton Road after shopping expeditions with my mother and gazing down at this little pub. On the opposite corner was the Diadem Flour Company, the premises of which are now home to Infix Ltd.

A well-dressed class of children at Easton Road school in the 1920s. A variety of styles are on show here including Eton and sailor collars and frilled pinafores.

Class 6 pictured in 1930 or 1931. Joan Ward is in the front row, second from left.

Inside the school during the 1930s. In the background can be seen the sliding doors which divided up the classrooms – a popular device of the time as more space could be provided when needed by pulling back the doors.

Another choice class from te same decade posing self-consciously with their exercise books.

Two delightful pictures showing pupils Maypole dancing in 1930. Harry Ward is among the group but I wonder if anyone else recognises themselves in their white May Day garb?

The dancing is about to begin. One wonders how white their clothes were by the end of the day!

An elegant Lena Barnes stands beside her husband Jack's car outside their Park Row home during the 1940s. The car's mudguards and running board have been painted white – a necessary safety precaution when adhering to the black-out regulations in the Second World War.

Outside the New Inn, Leadhouse Road around 1960, are the landlord Mr Stubbins, Bob Stubbins and friends.

Inside the pub, celebrations are in progress after a sporting victory in the 1960s.

Easton Road school stands almost alone with only a couple of vacated houses in Hulbert Street for company around 1974.

Properties in Easton Road take their final bow while those still standing were once Helps the grocers, Teleradio, The Marlborough and a house belonging to a Kestor Ford. The house at the back of the gap is that from which Lines Taxis were run.

The same scene from a different angle as more masonary crashes down with accompanying clouds of dust

A close up of the Lines' house, No. 30 which was originally a farmhouse dating from the seventeenth century, and ruthlessly razed in 1965.

Looking towards Clarence Road from the corner of Hulbert Street shows a depressing view of boarded up shops, pubs and the Salvation Army citadel, still in 1965.

Diary of destruction – the relentless inroads being made into Nos 37-43 Easton Road, reducing to rubble once-loved family homes in 1965. The only cheery note is Rolf Harris smiling down from a hoarding, advertising peaches on the side wall of Peg's café. This is the section between Stanley Street and Thrissell Street where the Leisure Centre is now located. A beautiful Gothic porch is about to meets its end at No. 37.

Only No. 37 left now. The chimneys in the background belong to the houses in Thrissell Street which faced the factory.

Another view of the tearing down of Nos 37-43.

Some of the new housing has been built. Soon the other vacated spaces will bear the imprint of a planner's scheme. The notion of modern housing with hot water and inside lavatories was undeniably a splendid concept but many aspects were overlooked. Tower block living proved an isolating experience and lack of amenities, even the most basic such as handy shops, gave an impersonal feel to the scheme. The community spirit was undermined.

Some of the last pupils to attend the school stand by the Boy's Entrance – a reminder of days when boys and girls were segregated.

The contrast of early seventies fashions against the old, soon-to-be-replaced school is interesting especially when viewed in comparison to playground groups from earlier decades shown in this chapter.

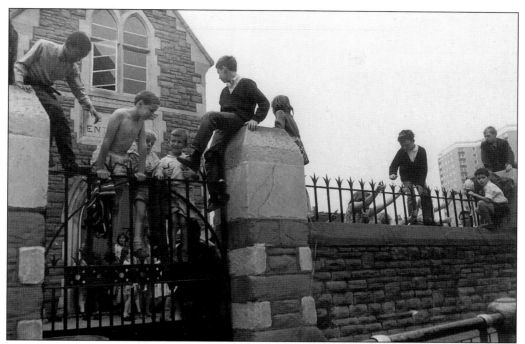

Playtime and the children expend their energy climbing the walls and the apparatus. They will all be grown up with children of their own by now.

The children take advantage of the apparatus. Where are they now and do they have any memories of this little area, so vastly altered?

Time to go home. The school had become almost an island by this time with just a few derelict shops in Easton Road left as neighbours.

The last few stragglers leave for home and the last few buildings on Easton Road – those from Allwood's cake shop to the Albion on the corner of Leigh Street – are dwarfed against the new multi-storey flats during the late 1960s.

A look back in time to how things once were – Joan Ward's class in the early 1930s. How saddened they must have felt when the old school finally fell.

A typical little 1950s off-licence punctuating a terrace of houses, their front doors opening directly onto the street. This one stood in Thrissell Street. When streets like these were replaced with modern housing it was not deemed necessary, apparently, to provide the residents with shops.

The cobbled thoroughfare that was Gladstone Street where a street party celebrating VE Day is in progress.

Little Victoria Street's residents who have really gone to town on the flags on Coronation Day, June 1953. The backs of the houses in the distance are those of Twinnell Road.

Residents tuck into the refreshments, June 1953. Why the tank of fish? Were they afraid the food would run out?

Years have passed by and the residents meet up again for a reunion. Someone has managed to save the street name plate, but all else disappeared in the 1960s.

A view from Twinnell House as Easton Way takes shape around 1970. Day's Road gasworks can be glimpsed in the background.

A bird's eye view of Easton Road school and the terrace between Leigh Street and Park Street again taken from Twinnell House around 1970.

Located next to St Lawrence's church was Mr Poole's chemist's shop. Nothing was too much trouble for him and he frequently made up medicines for sufferers out of pharmacy hours.

Almost opposite was this pub – the Wellesley Arms. This was sacrificed for the redevelopment programme in the first years of the 1960s.

A little further along stood Emma Counter's greengrocery business pictured in the late 1920s. Emma's son, Charles, stands in the doorway. Next door is the Victory pub which was run originally by the Fosketts and later by Edward Bennett. This land is now covered by the outer perimeter of the Lawrence Hill roundabout.

The Counter sisters, Emma's daughters, from left to right: Joyce, Win, Doreen, Ada and Alice in 1939.

# *Three*
# St Gabriel's

*St Gabriel's – the very name conjures up images of lantern slides in the church, the smell of chalk dust and ink wells in the school and playing marbles in the corridors in wet playtimes. The church was a focal point in the community and provided plenty of social activity, especially for the young people. Even today the Scout group is still going strong with yesterday's children as today's leaders although it is nearly thirty years since the red-brick Victorian church was pulled down.*

Mr and Mrs Stone of No. 201 Easton Road pictured in the 1940s. The family were well-known local coal dealers.

St Gabriel's Scouts strike camp under the leadership of Mr Gullick in the 1930s. In the back row on Mr Gullick's left is Bill Williams who later joined the army. The Gullicks had a daughter called Margaret. Harry Ward is also a member of this group.

The scouts, c. 1935-1936. From left to right, back row: Tincklin, Lloyd, Lloyd, Payne, Garmston, Wiltshire, Stacey. Middle row: Potter, Allen, Williams, Mr Hayden (scoutmaster), Garmston, Monks, Thomas. Front row: Haberfield, Chippett, Payne, Ward, Curtis.

St Gabriel's cricket team 1935. From left to right, back row: Mr Ellis, Haskins, Lovell, Cove, Thomas, Mountford, Mr Greenslade (headmaster). Middle row: Rowden, Havens, Luff (captain), Stacey, Kenna. Front row: Benjamin, Rogers.

Class 5, St Gabriel's c. 1931. The two staff members are Mr Francombe, the headmaster and Miss Johnson. From left to right, back row: Patten, Chippett, -?-, -?-, Garmston, Tucker, Bridle, Thomas, Barber. Middle row: Williams, Rudd, Lloyd, Harding, Flinders, -?-, Cullinane, -?-, Prigg, -?-, -?-, Allen. Second row: Watts, Stevens, Laver, Luff, Durston, Brewer, Pope, Gifford. Kneeling: Collins, Belcher, Harison, Jarrett, Denford, Rogers, Morris, West, Payne, Blackford. Front row: Rowden, Emery, -?-.

VE Day party on Lion Street. From left to right, middle row: Iris Davis, Maureen Harvey, Barbara Britton. Front row: Valerie Davis, Margaret Honey, Beryl Payne, Pearl Thatcher, Marlene Wheaton, John Eddolls, Jimmy Phillips, Christine Eddolls. At the back Vera Thatcher is holding one of her twin boys.

The middle of the 1960s marked the end of the old Easton as we knew it. Demolition began on a grand scale and scores of streets were removed from the map forever. This photograph from 1966, shows the back of the Lion public house, a small oasis in a desert of desolation. The houses in the background may be the remnants of Stork Street.

Inside the Lion, a cosy place with its wood panelling, wrought iron work tables, highly polished woodwork and Victorian fireplaces. It was finally pulled down in the late 1960s.

In the lounge hung the dartboard over a rather interesting fireplace. Those were the days when an ashtray was standard equipment on every plain surface!

Miss Trugnell's class at St Gabriel's, 1925. It is interesting to witness the grown-up fashions of the day reflected in the children's hairstyles and the girls' low-waisted dresses. Miss Bishop is the other teacher in the photograph. Among the children are Doreen (Ethel) Thomas, Edna Mole, George Smailes, Iris Mann, George Flinders, Irene Gooding, Violet McAuliffe, Pearl Benjamin, Toy Brewer, Hilda Griffin, Iris Richards, Dorothy Pope and Iris Sweet.

The girls in Form III, Doreen Thomas in the centre. Also included are Ivy Harrison and Joyce Dyte.

Class VI in 1931 includes Doreen Thomas, Vera Scorey, Pearl Benjamin, Irene Morris, Doris Lyddon, Eileen Watkins, Ivy Furlong, Edna Edgar, Dorothy Pope, Ruth Sumner, Joyce Dyte and May Cooper. Miss Mountstevens is the teacher and the headmistress, Mrs Coram is on the right. She taught the class to sing the French national anthem.

The Captain Ball team in 1934; Doreen, as captain, sits in the centre. Miss Snell and Miss Neal are the staff and among the team are Doris Stevens, Irene Patten, Iris Mann and Joan Lewis.

A segment of Easton Road prior to 1964. These shops, Nos 111-115, were in the rank between Twinnell Road and Twinnell Street which was comprised of a mixture of houses and shops. There was also a pub called the Talbot. These shops faced the old Croydon Street which lay slightly to the left of the present street line.

Roger and Peter Tovey pose with their pals, the Darnleys (Bruce, Richard and John) and Roger Cave in the yard behind the fish shop around 1950. The roofs of Seal Street can be seen in the background.

Roger, Peter and Bob the dog play by the cockle shed around the 1950s.

Roger (back right) with a group of friends in Lion Street also in the 1950s. The lad at the back is Trevor Cooper and behind him and to his left are the Darnley boys. Robert Gibbard is at the back with Roger Cave in front. The remaining boy is a visitor from Frampton Cotterell, Paul Skidmore.

In Stapleton Road was one of those elegant houses which stood in the rank between Felix Road and Little Victoria Street near the position now occupied by Twinnell House. It is a Christmas morning in th early 1950s and Mr Cooper and his daughter Grace are entertaining guests. These houses were beautifully proportioned and had exceptionally fine doorways as can be seen in this photograph.

An unknown family photographed by William Franklyn of Twinnell Road between 1900-1920. This picture came into the possession of the author from her uncle's collection when he died but, sadly there was no clue as to the names of these people. Can anyone recognise a relative among this group?

Bouverie Street, 1947 where Bill Thomas can be seen giving his nephew Andrew a ride on his bike. There were two distinct styles of house in this street – flat fronted step-straight-into-the-street on one side and bay windowed with gardens on the other.

The public bar of the Union Tavern, seen here in 1965, stood on the corner of Twinnell Street and was one of the last buildings in the area to be pulled down.

Love's young dream – Pete Tovey and Susan Wellington, Easton Road in the 1950s.

Gwendoline Gore, who later became Mrs William Tovey, (back row, far left) is seen here among this group of smart local gas meter-readers in the 1940s.

Another look back at St Gabriel's where class VI A includes Doris Cave, Evelyn Selman, Joyce Wade, Irene Morris and Vera Scorey. Doreen Thomas is standing at the back by the map. The year is 1932.

In 1933 Class VI B show off their needlework.

A class of St Gabriel's from the 1950s with one girl wearing a 'waspie' belt which was the height of chic at the time.

The Thatcher twins – Barry and Roger – of Lion Street with their St Gabriel's class mates, c. 1950. Paul Collins is almost certainly standing at the back, third from right in the sharp suit.

# Four
# All Hallows

Most of the houses lost in this area were sacrificed for educational purposes. Houses in Graham Road, Bannerman Road and Normanby Road were on land used by Bannerman Road school which was expanded, due to the increasing number of children in the district. Now the old school itself will soon vanish too as the new school rises beside it. Sadly the old Victorian edifice had outlived its usefulness and another era ends.

Bannerman Road School Football team 1948/49. From left to right, back row: Mr Butcher (sports master), Colin Bell, Colin Ball, John Thompson, John Hacker, Colin Haynes, Tony Reynolds, George Allen, Mr Lewis (headmaster). Middle row: (seated) Michael Always, Terry Warren, John Jordan, Leslie Snelling, David Plummer. The two boys sitting in the front are Michael Worlock and Barry Monks.

A VE Day party in All Hallows Road. The boys on the left in the front are Don Box, Terry Everson, and Derek Marsh and the lad in the front at the right is John Worlock. The group standing to the right are comprised of (from front) Phyllis Hucker, Mrs Gertie Box, Roy Clouter, Vera Marsh, Brian Cooper, Father Bedford. Esme Marsh can be seen at the far end of the table on the right, seated. Those standing to the left include Mrs Batt, Mrs Marsh, Mrs Worlock and Mrs Williams. The Co-op building can be seen in the background.

Britannia Road residents celebrate the end of the Second World War. From left to right: Mrs Parsons, Mrs Lewis, Kathleen Haines, Mary Wooldridge, Thelma Bennett, -?-, Mrs Porter, Mrs Johnson, -?-.

A bus outing organized by the residents of Britannia Road, c. 1948-1949. Some of the 'trippers' have been identified: Mr Long is on the left wearing a white shirt and standing in front of him is Richard Haines. Peggy Brown is on the left at the back and Kathleen Haines is in front of the middle window. Looking out of the window is Mr Wooldridge and Mrs Wooldridge is behind the man holding the spade – identified as Mr Brown. Tommy Wooldridge is on the far right. Mrs Arbury is in the centre wearing a cardigan and Ann Haines is next to her in a patterned dress and dark hat.

Alan Ballinger and fellow All Hallows scouts enjoy themselves on a trip to London in July 1965.

The boys pose outside the church.

Little Geoffrey Lawrence, armed and dangerous in All Hallows Road, during the 1950s. Since the time of this photograph the garages and houses have gone, to be replaced by modern flats called St Gabriel's Court. The wall on the right-hand side (just visible) has also disappeared along with the houses to which they belonged as Bannerman Road school expanded over the years until it was decided to build a replacement school in 2001.

Bannerman Road school in 1939 and the windows have already been taped to prevent the glass shattering in the event an explosion from bombing attacks during the Second World War.

A local football team which included Bill Harris, (three rows back on the left), but who were they? Perhaps some reader might recognise themselves or a relative.

Young Graham Haynes, the butcher's son, from No. 93 Chelsea Road plays in the cab of the wagon belonging to John Harris owner of the coal yard at No. 95, during the 1920s. Graham was sadly a casualty of the Second Wolrd War.

Harris' yard was perfect for all sorts of excitement and games. Here Avis Howes plays in a beautifully crafted toy car against the background of Chelsea Road houses, those between Britannia Road and Bloy Street. Avis was the daughter of Dennis Howes who ran the newsagent at No. 91 Chelsea Road. The fashions reflect the period of the 1920s.

Young Graham again – this time astride the horse who pulled the coal cart, again from the 1920s. He loved horses and spent every available moment in the yard. Harris' coal yard was established around 1900. The family also ran the shop next door as a general store selling everything from the horsemeat to ice-cream. European officials would probably haev something to say about this combination today!

One of the Harris boys who has obviously been grooming the horse which looks in splendid condition.

Archie Harris, who ran an ice cream business from his father's shop at No. 95 Chelsea Road, is seen here preparing a new batch. The recipe was a closely guarded secret which unfortunately died with him. His brother, Fred, is just visible in the top left-hand corner, overseeing the operation.

Three of the Harris children intheir Sunday best at th rear of the coal yard around 1914. They are, in descending order, Edward, Edie and Bill. In later years John Harris rented out the yard but retained the shop. When he finally retired he became caretaker of Whitehall cahpel on the corner of Woodbine Road.

The demolition of the end cottages in Albion Road in the late 1960s. They stood where the small park is now.

Mr and Mrs Ernest Chapman in their Lena Street garden with a wonderful collection of moving garden ornaments which he made. They lived here from the 1920s-1940s and this photograph is probably from the late 1930s.

Mr Green's class from February 1952. Back row, from left to right:-?-, Michael Rossiter, Peter Hoskins,-?-,-?-,-?-,-?-,-?-. Middle row, from left to right: Michael Mott, Kenneth Page, Anita ?, Joy Daw, Diane Payne, Sandra ?, Kathleen ?, Janet Cooling, Pat Cottle,-?-,-?-. Front row, from left to right: Marlene Griffiths,-?-, Sandra Sparrow, Margaret Tinkling, Joan Pike, Valerie Kelly, Barbara Yelland, Dawn lynus, Maureen ?, Sheila Wriggly and Sheils ?

Ann Lawrence is just about to step on the balancing board ina Physical Training exercise from around 1950. The houses seen in the background are those in Bannerman Road, which were pulled down for the building of Spring Woods Nursery School.

A Banerman Road school class from the 1950s which includes Michael Mott, (back row, third from right). More Bannerman Road houses in the background which no longer exist.

Sylvia Ballinger queues in Charlie Wilcox's chip shop which used to stand in the rank between The Queen's Head, Easton Road and Wright Place. The post office was also sited here until the 1960s when it relocated to Bannerman Road and now occupies premises once used as a butcher's shop.

Bessie Carter who used to live with her parents at No. 212 Easton Road during the 1930s-40s and worked at Packer's chocolate factory. Her training in the St John's Ambulance service meant neighbours were calling on her at all hours for help and advice. Those were pre-NHS days when doctors' fees were a deterrent to all but the most necessary visits to the surgery.

Bloy street residents celebrate the Queen's Silver Jubilee in 1977. In the bottom picture Nick Campbell sits at the table to the right of the balloon. All the houses in shot have been replaced by modern buildings.

In the bottom picture Nick Campbell sits at the table to the right of the balloon. All the houses to the right have been replaced by modern buildings. Nick's grandmother, Mrs Crane, is in the centre of the top photograph, wearing the tam o'shanter and plaid and is dancing to the piper's tune. (Her daughter, Janet's wedding is seen on page 101).

Bannerman Road pupils in 1906. The boys seem to be wearing more lace than the girls!

The year is 1944 and the Boys Brigade are seen marching round the corner past the Owen Street Mission into Chelsea Road. The gardens on the right belong to a terrace which has since been demolished in favour of more modern housing and the buildings on the left part of Owen Square have gone to be replaced by a park. The band march in the direction of Albion Road and Roman Road.

# Five
# St Anne's

People came from all around to work at the chocolate factory where use of local labour was always the company policy. This was not a district which boasted a main shopping area. Here it was corner shops and off-licences and the occasional small rank of traders providing staple goods.

London House during the 1950s, which stood on the corner of Russell Town Avenue and Proctor Street – an area now covered by St George School playing fields.

Another pub which disappeared around the same time was the Prince of Wales which was located in the corner of Cattybrook Street and Russell Town Avenue next to the City Mission. At the time of this photograph from the 1950s the landlady was Elizabeth Jane Isaacs.

The Warn family. Mrs Eliza Warn traded as a grocer at Nos 193 and 195 Whitehall Road from the early part of the twentieth century until the 1950s. In later years her son, William George, used part of the premises for his window display sign business. Mrs Warn is seated, to the left, in a white blouse. Her husband, William Henry, is standing back left wearing a top hat. Her son William is in the front in a sailor suit. The whole family are gathered in the garden behind the shop on this summer's day in 1907.

The Whitehall Road Co-op, in the 1920s. This has now been converted into offices.

The King's Head as it was prior to the First World War when Frederick Parsons was the landlord around 1920.

VE Day party at the Croft's End Mission. It looks as if they may have run out of chairs!

St Ambrose Girl Guides pictured in the 1960s. Maureen Sibley is in the front row, second from right. Maureen is the granddaughter of Emma Counter whose shop can be seen on page 46.

The Prince of Wales off-licence in Gordon Road in the 1960s. It has since been converted into a private dwelling.

A mystery photograph which looks as though it was taken outside a sports pavilion. I would be interested to hear from anyone who could shed any light on this?

Packers chocolate factory in the early years of the twentieth century. Those flounced pinafores must have been cumbersome garments to work in!

The packing room around 1910; it must have been cold in there as all the men are wearing hats.

Dinner break and the lads tuck into their grub, possibly bread and dripping.

The laboratory where new flavours were constantly being tried and assessed. When I worked there in later years I always volunteered to be on the tasting panel!

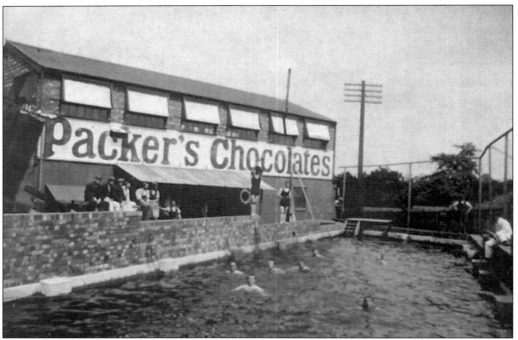

What better way to spend your break on a hot day than having a dip in the pool?

The works canteen, *c.* 1950s.

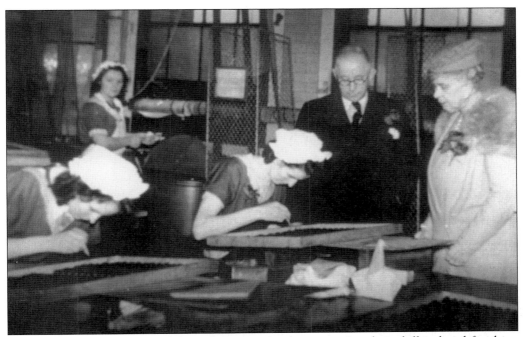

A visit from Queen Mary and the girls seem to be demonstrating their skill in hand-finishing chocolates.

The box-making room. In the 1950s-1960s the manager was Frank Johnson. His wife, Joyce, was secretary to the buyer, the kindly and well-respected Bert Wreyford, who was a cricket fanatic.

The hauling way in the days before it was not considered unhygienic to have horses wandering about next to sacks of sugar awaiting processing.

One of the production departments with the wooden trays stacked ready to cool the sweets.

Bindler – the revolutionary German machine designed to speed up production. The girl with dark hair is Yvonne Swann.

These ladies appear to be packing liqueurs

Co-op stores sprung up like mushrooms in the early years of the twentieth century but lost out in the supermarket wars of the 1960s. This rather lovely building on the corner of Greenbank Road and Kingsley Road is now used as offices.

This shop, on the Emlyn/Greenbank Road corner served as a dairy for many years beginning in the 1920s. It was run first by Frederick Wilcox and later by Stanley Line. It met the fate of so many corner shops by being converted for domestic use in 2000.

Leslie Norman's class at Greenbank Infants' school, *c.* 1921. Leslie is seated two in front of the girl standing by the radiator with her doll.

Three years on and Leslie is now in Miss Briggs' class.

Standard 8 in the 1930s. The teacher here is John C. Iles and the headmaster, standing at the back, is Norman Savory.

VE Day party in Carlyle Road. It looks as if everyone has been prevailed upon to bring out their best dining room chairs.

It is now 1953 and a Coronation Party is in progress in Tudor Road. The boy in the pram is Alan Cowley and the little chap with ER emblazoned on his chest is John Wyatt. Lillian Phelps and Molly White are amongst the revellers.

Anstey Street where there was also a party going on in 1953. The Sutton sisters, Doreen and Audrey, are in fancy dress. Doreen is rigged out as a bathing belle and cheeky Audrey is the Queen of Po-Land.

The girls are joined by other contestants – next to Audrey (far left) is Mrs Holmyard, then Mrs Williams, Mrs Hardwick, Mrs Middle and the girls' mum, Mrs Sutton.

John and Keith Johnson of No. 57 Anstey Street getting in the party spirit.

The Easton Weslyan church is now a Gospel church. In the 1920s the Pastor was Walter Daddow and, as can be seen by this page from the church magazine, a large number of local people were involved in the many activities provided.

One popular activity was membership of the drama society known as The Tudor Players. They were a very professional group and their productions drew large crowds. Here *Aladdin* is being staged in 1947. The actors involved were Alfie Rooks, Bob Smith, Gloria Gaydon, Peter Gunning, Roy Cowley, June Perrett and Pat Baker.

# Six

# St Mark's

*The structural changes have not been so great here but the atmosphere is very different. Gone are all the little drapery stores, clothes shops, tobacconists and the grocery shops with their overwhelming smells of broken biscuits and salty bacon. Instead it has become the epicentre for exotic foods and oriental spices. The place teems with life and won a Civic award in 1996.*

This would have been the view from the Warwick Road corner around the time of the First World War. The fine houses on the right were demolished in the 1980s and replaced with modern housing. Those to the left, of an earlier period, thankfully remain.

A busy little scene further down towards the railway arch where there was once a cluster of little shops – newsagent, milliner, greengrocery, jeweller. Shopping around 1920 was a daily, often sociable event, quite different from thr fraught weekly supermarket stock-up so common in today's society.

Frederick Ellery's bakery shop in the 1920s which stood on the Berwick Road corner of St Mark's Road. In the 1940s this became a second hand shop known as *Winnie's* as it was run by Winifred Hewlett.

A portrait of Harold Walker and his wife of St Mark's Road in the 1920s. In the early days of radio he became an enthusiast and built his own wireless sets on which he even managed to pick up American stations!

Patsy Chinn and Margaret Sheppard of Lena Street enjoying an afternoon out in the sun during the 1940s.

Mivart Street in the 1940s. Something of interest is going on at the top of the street to judge by the little huddles of people gathered to watch.

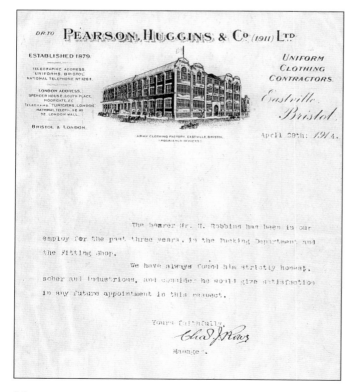

A reference from Pearson, Huggins and Co. (1911) Ltd, typed on their impressive notepaper. It is more usually now referred to as 'the Epstein Building' after the picture framers who later occupied the premises. It is now divided up into units, many of them used as studios. One of which produces work under the 'Fetish' label.

The Majoti family in the first shop they opened in St Mark's Road trading as Bristol Sweet Mart in the 1970s. They have since expanded dramatically and now trade world wide on the internet. Sons Abdul Ismail, Yunas, Saleem, Rashid and daughter Hamida are also invloved in the business, making it a real family concern.

Dave Lewis's mini-market shortly before it closed in the 1980s. The shop had been in the Lewis family since the 1930s prior to which it had been Trubody's Grocery Store. In the 1970s the shop was extended by buying up Edbrooks, the butcher's shop next door. Hibbert's continus to flourish as does Big Saver next door.

S. Loxton.

St Mark's church seen from the Albion Road/High Street corner before the railway line was extended and the cottages demolished to accommodate the enlargement of the embankment. The buildings on the corner of High Street are seen here as private dwellings. Later structural alterations changed their purpose to that of shops. The church has been transformed into a hostel in recent years.

The altar of St Mark's church decorated for the Harvest Festival of 1941. Bombs might be raining down but traditions were still observed!

Members of the Mother's Union face the camera in the vicarage grounds in the 1940s. Mrs Parsons is on the far left and Mrs Chinn second from right.

The St Mark's Girls' club in 1938 on what looks like a rather chilly day out. Patsy Chinn is the girl in front, on the right.

The girsl pose precariously on a five-bar gate. Patsy is third from left. In the 1930s they would have been classed as 'junior misses', rather than teenagers.

How we all used to love a wedding. Everyone used to gather at the gates to admire the bride who, in this case, was Janet Crane of Bloy Street on her way up St Mark's church path to become Mrs Campbell in 1959.

Cover of the programme for the 1978 memorial service of George Stubbs, vicar of St Mark's for twenty-six years. His grave in the grounds of the church was tended faithfully by his widow, Christina until she died in 1993.

Perkins building in St Mark's Road which incorporated the Manor House used as a YMCA in the 1920s and '30s. It was demolished in the early 1990s in favour of modern housing.

The corner of Lawrence Avenue, 1980s. The tobbacconist's shop on the corner which used to be Eastlake's is being used a second hand shop and Cannocks still trade on the opposite corner. Nirwan Fabrics are in the shop which was once Beadle's the cobbler and also a hairdressing salon run by Janet Smeaton whose parents kept a grocery shop at No. 50 St Mark's Road for many years. Next door Saleem Akhtar has begun trading in what has been Jessica's draper shop.

Christmas 1949 and pupils of Mrs Lake's secretarial school, Rene Road, gather at All Hallows hall for their annual party accompanied by their partners. Doreen Sutton is in the front, far right.

Nos 27 and 29 St Mark's Road in the late 1980s. The shop called 'Gear Change' - run as a 'as-new' concern by Fiona Cockell - had formerly been Naylor's hardware shop. After Fiona gave up the tenancy the shop was converted into two flats and Easton lost yet another corner shop.

The author's family on the steps of her grandmother's house, with visitors from Plymouth shortly to be leaving from Stapleton Road station in 1961. Perkins' shop can be seen looming behind with the small building next door which served a variety of purposes over the years from TV rental company to sign manufacturers.

The author walking on the park which was created when twelve houses and a shop in Belmont Street were pulled down for a scheme which was later abandoned. Since the time of this photograph in the mid-1980s the last of the old houses which backed on to Belmont Street has gone, being replaced by modern housing. The pub, the South Wales Railway Tavern, had also disappeared. Flats are being built on the site.

Details of the auction in 1937 when the YMCA building and various properties which the organization owned were sold.

By Order of the Trustees.

# EASTON.

### IMPORTANT SALE BY AUCTION OF

Lot 1.—

## AN EXTENSIVE BLOCK OF FREEHOLD BUILDINGS

### and an adjoining UNCOVERED SITE in

## ST. MARK'S ROAD, EASTON

### *(With Vacant Possession).*

Having together an approximate

### Site Area 2,255 Square Yards,

and for many years used as the

### EAST BRISTOL Y.M.C.A.,

comprising:—
CONCERT HALL—LIBRARY—RECEPTION ROOMS—GAMES ROOMS—BUFFET—BOARD and COMMITTEE ROOMS—ADMINISTRATIVE OFFICES—BILLIARD ROOMS—GYMNASIUMS — Fitted Bath and Cloakrooms. (Hot Water Radiators and Domestic Supply from Specially Installed Coke Boilers). GARAGE and CYCLE SHEDS.

### *Free from Ground Rent.*

Lot 2.—

**37, ST. MARK'S ROAD, EASTON.**
Let to Mr H. Lewis at the inclusive rent of 12/6 weekly. Annual Rent Charge £3

Lot 3.—

**39, ST. MARK'S ROAD, EASTON.**
Until recently let at the inclusive rent of 16/- weekly. **THE PROPERTY IS NOW VACANT.** Annual Rent Charge £3 4s

Lot 4.—

**23, BELMONT STREET, EASTON.**
Let to Mr Shelper at the inclusive rent of 15/- weekly. Annual Rent Charge £1 10s.
**(NOTE.—This Property is Registered as Decontrolled).**

Lot 5.—

**24, BELMONT STREET, EASTON.**
Let to Mr H. Pearce at the inclusive rent of 15/- weekly. FREE FROM GROUND RENT.

Lot 6.—

**9, ST. MARK'S GROVE EASTON.**
Let to Mr Allen at the inclusive rent of 10/6 weekly. Annual Rent Charge £3 3s.

which

# STANLEY ALDER & PRICE

Have been instructed to OFFER FOR SALE by AUCTION, at THE WHITE SWAN HOTEL, EAST-VILLE, on WEDNESDAY, April 28th, 1937, at Seven o'clock in the Evening.

Printed Particulars and Conditions of Sale, with Plans, can be obtained from the Auctioneers, as above, "Estate Buildings," 7, St. Stephen's Street, Bristol. Tel. 20301 (two lines), and 94c, Whiteladies Road, Clifton. Tel. 34394; or from

Messrs H. B. NISBET & CO., Solicitors.
47, Mecklenburgh Square, London, W.C.1.

A group leaving one of the many afternoon meetings which were held at the YMCA. The organization used the old manor house as its headquarters and part of the ground floor was used as a school for a while. The building stretched from St Mark's Road to the back of the houses in Belmont Street with its side wall in St Mark's Grove. The blonde boy standing woith his mother by the railings is Dennis Rugman who lived in one of the cottages in Albion Road which can be seen part demolished on poage 69.

105

The YMCA were allowed to use the grounds of Ridgeway House in Fishponds as a sports ground. Here a group relax in the shade during a cricket match. Lionel Ellery is on the left wearing a cap.

The caretaker of the YMCA, Rupert Ellery, was allowed to use the wasteland between the building and Belmont Street to grow vegetables and keep chickens. Here he leans on a spade perhaps instructing his youngest son Don on one of the finer points of poultry keeping.

Rupert Ellery and wife Jane pose on the waste ground which extended as far as St Nicholas' Park , the houses of which can be seen to the right. With them are sons Denis and Lionel (sporting rather impressive headgear) and youngest daughter Iris. The photograph dates from 1929. Iris died the following winter.

Jane Ellery and son Denis have a souvenir snapshot taken with some Dunkirk survivors to whom they offered hospitality as they passed through Bristol en route to Tyneside.

A very dapper Ted Wootten poses in his garden in Nicholas Road in the 1920s; what an elegant cane!

Michael Benson in his smart little racing car, Nicholas Road, 1935.

The St John Ambulance station, formerly the local labour exchange on the corner of Woodborough Street and St Mark's Road. This was demolished in the 1990s so that flats could be built on the site.

Hancocks carpet shop at No. 252 Stapleton Road in the 1970s. Prior to that it belonged to the Co-operative Society, and is now an international call centre.

Margaret Hoare, who worked as an assistant to Mr Philpott, a very kindly chemist, always willing to impart advice during the 1950s. Margaret's family lived in the flat over the shop so you can be sure she was never late for work!

Margaret and the senior assistant Miss Harvey, *c.* 1956. A lot of time must have been spent preparing the window display.

Roger Tovey displaying a magnificent Sturgeon which is now stuffed and on display at the Manor House Hotel, Castle Combe. Stapleton Road looks relatively quiet on this day in 1972.

Roger is joined by his father outside their shop. In the background is the Lebeck (now Lebeq's Tavern) with the relatively new Twinnell House towering behind.

The Cottles' house which stood alongside the lane which ran from Chaplin Road to Bannerman Road. The lane can just be seen to the left. The photograph dates from the late 1960s, just prior to demolition. There was a strip of waste ground to the rear of the property where a segment of Bannerman Road houses had been demolished in the 1950s.

The same house seen from a different angle on the same day. The remaining houses in this section of Bannerman Road were lost at this time and the site used to build Spring Woods nursery school. The houses to the left are those in Normanby Road. The even numbers were pulled down around 1974 to provide a playing field for Bannerman Road school.

# Seven

# St Thomas'

*Not all these photographs are strictly in the parish of St Thomas as some parts are in the parish of Stapleton, which always delighted many as getting married at Stapleton church carried a certain amount of prestige. Eastville Park has always dominated this area, together with the slopes of Purdown so those children who lived in the area were fortunate indeed as they could go boating on the lake, catch tiddlers and tadpoles in the river and have picnics on Purdown. In addition there were lanes behind the houses with trees to climb and a railway embankment to scramble up; the children who lived here never knew boredom!*

Doris Wootten married an Australian soldier, Roy Benson, at St Thomas church, c. 1920.

Eastville Club members armed with their cues and ready to take on any challenge in the 1940s.

The Eastville Division of the British Legion on a ceremonial occasion in the 1940s.

...re invited to attend a

28

# Grand Billiards and Snooker Exhibition
## at The Eastville Club
### (ENTRANCE TO EASTVILLE STADIUM)
## on Monday — 23rd April, 1945.
THE PROCEEDS WILL BE DEVOTED TO THE EVENING WORLD SECTION
OF THE BRISTOL'S OWN FUND
# Mr. JOE DAVIS,
*(World Snooker Champion and Billiards Champion of Great Britain)*
WILL ENGAGE CLUB MEMBERS IN GAMES OF BILLIARDS AND SNOOKER
**First Game starts at 6.45 p.m.**

THIS CARD IS AN ACKNOWLEDGMENT OF YOUR DONATION OF **7/6** TO THE B.O.F.

During the evening Mr. Davis will conduct an auction of articles presented by generous
donors throughout the city for this special fund

**ADMISSION BY CARD ONLY**

A special treat at the Eastville Club in 1945 when Joe Davies, later to become a popular TV
personality, threw down the gauntlet to members of the Billiards and Snooker club.

The Rovers ground was used for diverse purposes; here in 1918, a whist drive is in progress.
The houses in the background are those in what the locals called The Lower Road. It was
in fact a continuation of Stapleton Road. These properties were demolished for the building
of the M32.

Coombe Road School, *c.* 1935. In the back row, third from right is Allen Hopton who sadly died when he was eight when complications set in after suffering from scarlet fever.

The King family – Tom, his wife Margaret and daughters Betty and Annie around the 1920s. Mr King ran Monarch Coaches at Eastville, using premises beside the Black Swan.

The slopes of Purdown held a magnetic attraction for the young. Youngsters would slide down in snowy weather and use the upper ridge as a vantage point on Guy Fawkes night to watch the *Evening Post*'s firework display at the Rovers' ground for free. Doreen Thomas and friends spend an afternoon there in the 1930s. In the background can be seen the new houses in Sir John's Lane.

Time now to join the Home Guard, Tackley Road division at their 'stand down' dinner in 1944.

An average crowd at the Rovers' ground in the 1950s. On Saturday afternoons when the team was playing at home, thousands of spectators would swarm through the streets of Eastville towards the stadium; it was like a scene from *Close Encounters*. As can be seen here the vast majority of the men wore flat caps and long macs.

The Rovers' line-up in the 1950s. Back row, from left to right: J. Pitt, H. Banford, H. Hoyle, G. Fox, V. Lambden, P. Sampson. Front row, from left to right: G. Petherbridge, G. Bradford, R. Warren (Capt.), W. Roost, J. Watling.

Many hold fond memories of the Bristol Rover Supporters' Club, shown here around 1960.

**BRISTOL ROVERS
FOOTBALL CLUB** Nº 06633
**LIMITED**

# SOUTH STAND

Block "B" Row K Seat No. 33

MATCH: v ASTON VILLA

DATE: 14 SEP 1974

PRICE : ~~80p~~ £1.00

*E P Terry*

SECRETARY

Ticket to a Bristol Rovers game in 1974. Prices were a little different then!

Freemantle Road in days gone by. This musical ensemble are gathered in the garden of No. 18 during the 1930s.

Freemantle Road in later years during the removal of property for road widening, c. 1970.

'Lower' Stapleton Road after the removal of the side of even-numbered houses. The struts are in place for the covering of the River Frome.

The end for the rank of houses Nos 472-502 Stapleton Road. In this section lived Bert Tann, manager of Bristol Rovers; his wife practiced as a chiropodist.

September 1945 and VE Day celebrations are the order of the day for these residents of Dormer Road and Rousham Road.

A VJ party being held by residents of Dormer Road and Rousham Road.

Here the ladies appear to be putting the finishing touches to costumes. From left to right: Mrs Sawyer, -?-, Mrs Mahoney, Mrs Fisher, Dawn Sawyer, Mrs Heyward.

This seems to be the organization committee for the Dormer Road/Rousham Road Coronation Party. From left to right, standing: -?-, Mr Sawyer, Mr Fisher, Mr Heyward. Seated: Mrs Sawyer, -?-, Mrs Mahoney, Mrs Fisher. Mrs Heyward, Dawn Sawyer.

The majority of the local children attended Coombe Road school. This picture was taken around 1947. A few years later Glenfrome School opened to cope with the post-war baby boom.

Miss Larkins' class from Eastville Girls' school assemble on the Centre for a school trip to London, 1949. The queue is headed by Doreen Sutton. Amongst the group are Margaret Norton, Mavis Williams, Shirley Beauchamp, Avril Cotter, Jean Good, Shirley Golledge, Joan Fowler and the Loche twins.

The staff netball team of Eastville girls' school. From left to right, back row: Miss Caple, Mrs Williams, Miss Sperrin, Mrs Harris. Front row: Mrs Smith, Mrs Johnson.

This more informal group are snapped on the same day in 1955. From left to right: Marian Caines, Mollie White, Pamela Abrahams, Mary Mart, Maureen Newman.

Miss Larkins' class of 1955. It is the end of Easter term and shows form 4.1.

The Endeavour netball team, 1955. From left to right, back row: D. Webb, Mollie White, Marian Caines, Maureen Newman. Front row: Vicky Pasker, S. Curtis, Margaret Hoare, Mary Mart.

Jack and the Beanstalk. Jack Hopton displays his prize veg in the garden of No. 11 Ingmire Road. The author's family lived at No. 12.

Margaret and Christine Hopton tend to the hens around 1946. The favourite was called Priscilla.

Harold and Grace Goodyear, relatives of the Hoptons who lived at the top end of Ingmire Road surrounded by family and friends. Jack Hopton was a builder and was responsible for the erection of some of the properties in the road which was unique in-as-much as it was paved with alternating pink and white slabs. The local children were inordinately proud of this fact.